The Neuroscience Of Dopamine Detox

Why Dopamine Fasting Usually Fails
And What To Do To Reset Your
Dopamine Levels, Take Back Control Of
Your Brain And End Laziness

Andrew Humington

i

Dear Reader,

Thank you for giving "The Neuroscience Of Dopamine Detox" a chance.

Before we dive in, we have some exclusive, unadvertised gifts just for you:

We, at the NeuroEducation Lab, would like to offer you these welcoming gifts to thank you for your trust and your love for neuroscience, and to help you make the most out of your potential.

The Checklist For Your Perfect Neuroscientific Morning Routine

To support you in your implementation of the strategies in "The Neuroscience of Morning Routines," we've created this easy-to-follow checklist to guide your morning routine.

Download It For Free At Neuromasterylab.com

Your Free Gift n°3:

Your free subscription to the Neuroeducation Lab VIP newsletter.

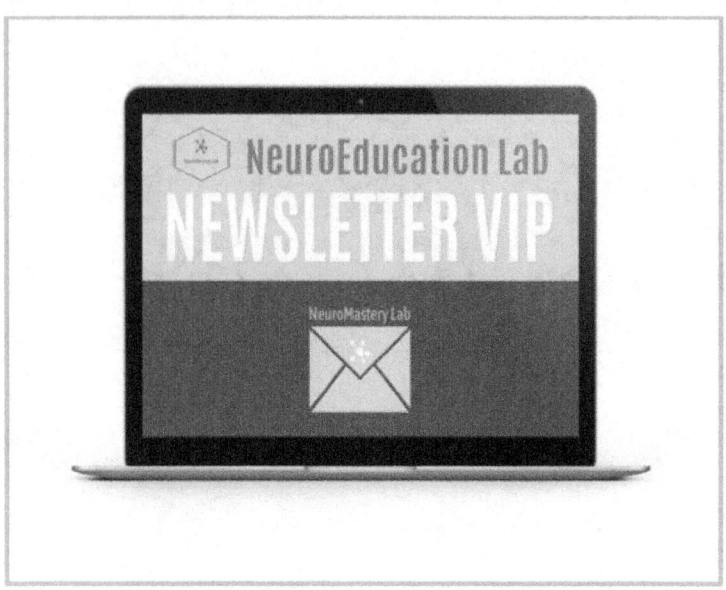

Stay updated with fascinating neuroscience findings and breakthroughs, helping you better understand yourself and your brain. Receive updates on our latest books and publications, along with access to launch pricing and exclusive, time-limited promotions.

Download It For Free At Neuromasterylab.com

Thank you again for your trust, we hope you'll enjoy all those "surprise" bonuses!

Now it's time to get started with the book:

Table of Contents

Chapter 1:
An Introduction to Dopamine Detox

Imagine a scenario of you scrolling through feeds and watching funny videos after a long day at work. Finally, after some time you put your phone down and realize that a whole hour has passed. You were meant to wash the dishes, put a load of washing on and start on dinner. Annoyed at yourself you vow to limit your social media consumption; however a few minutes later while looking for a good playlist to listen to, you hear a ping and see a notification come through that your favorite YouTuber has uploaded the latest episode in their gaming series. Excitement bubbles inside as you settle yourself to watch, household chores and your goal of limiting screen time forgotten.

Do you find yourself going through life, day after day, fixed in the same routine of activities that you used to find enjoyable and meaningful but now feel dull and boring? Procrastination has clouded your judgment and you are putting off completing important tasks on your to-do list and rather reaching for immediate sources of reward. Does your brain feel muddled by everything around you, that you do not know where to begin or even what brings you true gratification anymore? Knowing that you may be spending an unhealthy amount of time on activities that are not bettering you as a person, like watching YouTube videos or Netflix for numerous hours, but you cannot help yourself.

If this sounds like how you are feeling, you may benefit substantially from partaking in a dopamine detox.

The invention and development of technology in our modern life today have generated numerous advantages of keeping in touch with loved ones all over the world, staying up to date with current events that are happening as you read this book and even affording us the opportunity to continue working and studying if faced with events such as pandemics or protests. Unfortunately, like with all good things, technology also brings about disadvantages that have been proven to negatively affect our well-being. For many of us, our mobile phones are one of the first things we look at after waking up in the morning and have become an almost automatic "second limb" that we reach for when waiting in queues, trying to get out of awkward situations or to help the time go faster when completing household chores. As beneficial as this may be, having such easy access to devices that hold so much information is thought to mess with the reward center in our brains and affect how we see and feel about the real world. Regular experiences and interests that used to excite you will feel tedious and you will begin to lose any passion you once had for them.

This was the phenomenon that spurred Psychiatrist Dr. Cameron Sepah to hype up the dopamine detox.

What is Dopamine Detox, and why did it become such a popular trend?

In 2016, Greg Kamphuis prepared for a journey based on self-discovery aimed at reigniting his enthusiasm and establishing a meaningful life. He realized that he had become desensitized to real life and was not receiving any joy from experiences that had previously motivated him. Greg published his journal entries written during this time and reflected on them while describing what he believes daily life should look like. He links the release of dopamine to so-called "supernormal stimuli" by referencing experiments conducted by Nikolass Tinbergen who discovered that he could grab the attention of fish, birds, and male butterflies with supernormal stimuli. These are dramatized forms of natural stimuli and the animals he studied were observed to often favor the unnatural stimulus over the genuine one. Using these findings, Deirdre Barrett, a psychologist from Harvard University, proposed that supernormal stimuli may affect humans in similar ways.

This is where we bring in Dr. Sepah; after encountering one too many clients that were displaying signs of unhealthy behaviors that included reliance on their screens and social media, he created a method of treatment in an attempt to help these people essentially rewire their brains. He published an article entitled "Dopamine Fasting 2.0" in October 2019 and it quickly gained traction, becoming extremely popular with over 140 000 clicks and receiving coverage in a number of countries.

A dopamine detox consists of restricting activities, behaviors, and stimuli that you have identified as compulsive or that cause you to feel overwhelmed. The aim of this is to train your brain to not be dependent on these triggers by limiting the emotional effects that dopamine release causes and reestablishing flexibility over your behaviors. The behaviors and stimuli are restricted for a period of time, usually not indefinitely.

Dr. Sepah emphasized in his article that he is not handing over a list dictating what we should not be doing; this is instead for behaviors that we can identify as impairing, addictive and distressing. A behavior or stimulus can be described as impairing if it negatively interferes with daily functioning including home, social, work, and/or school life. For example, someone may go shopping almost every day and spend so much time in stores that it takes away from quality time with family or much-needed time they could have rather used to finish an important work project. We begin to see impulsive behavior eat into their optimal daily functioning. The development of addictive behaviors will be discussed in detail in the next chapter, but essentially these behaviors can be identified quite easily, and often people know they should stop, it is just extremely challenging to do so. Finally, a stimulus or behavior that is distressing will continuously generate negative emotions within you. You may feel good while participating in the activity, but as soon as it's finished and the "feel-good" effect has disappeared you clearly see it as a waste of time. If a stimulus or behavior can be described as one or more of the above, it is a perfect candidate to target in a dopamine detox.

Common myths and misconceptions about dopamine fasting

Unfortunately, with its rise in popularity, many people have misinterpreted what a dopamine detox really entails leading to doubts about the approach and resulting in negative connotations surrounding it.

Its first real supporters were mainly the so-called "tech-bros" of the Silicon Valley Bay Area which involved some people with radical ideas of the technique. For example, some people have gone to such extremes that they avoid forms of social interaction, including eye contact and talking, when partaking in their detox. This can actually have the opposite effect and be detrimental to their well-being because socializing is a natural and beneficial behavior for humans, even for people referred to as introverts or those who do not value relationships. Some extremists even give up healthy behaviors like exercise or reading for their detox.

It is important to note that dopamine detox is not a technique where you deprive yourself of all rewarding stimuli and behaviors. It is only those that you have identified as problematic for you and your functioning that you will limit. Dopamine detox also does not involve depriving yourself of all sources of stimulation; like talking, light stimulation, reading, music, eating, and exercise.

It is by no means intended to take over from religious practices such as asceticism or overseeing a Sabbath, it is also not a revamped version of mindfulness meditation. Dr. Sepah has warned against treating it like a vacation, as these are often the times when we are encouraged to indulge more in unhealthy behaviors. However, practicing meditation and going on intentional vacations during the detox are some ways in which you can have a more successful experience. More on this and other strategies in chapter four.

Although they are some of the people most in need of dopamine detox, this technique is not solely targeted to people in technologically heavy occupations. There are many unnatural sources of dopamine release; junk food, recreational drugs, shopping, alcohol, and gambling are just some behaviors that have the potential to become addictive and can be focused on during the dopamine detox.

Another misconception, and probably the most important one, stems from the name itself and not understanding the neurophysiology of dopamine. When hearing the term "Dopamine Detox," also sometimes referred to as a "Dopamine Fast," one may incorrectly assume the main aim is to decrease the levels of dopamine. These terms are misleading from a scientific point of view, although they do their job of grabbing people's attention and gaining publicity. Dopamine is essential for several functions and a fast from it would actually be harmful. More on this will be covered in the following chapter. Remember, what is actually being targeted is reducing behaviors identified as impulsive. Although both terms are used interchangeably, for the purpose of this book we will primarily use "Dopamine Detox."

We have set the stage for dopamine detox, learning briefly about its history, what it entails, and what it isn't. Now let's go into a more in-depth review of this popular trend. This book is going to cover the science of dopamine, how it functions, its pathways, and how exactly it is involved in the reward center of the brain. Next, we will dive into the benefits of dopamine detox and analyze if science agrees with the proposed advantages. The last two chapters will be your personal guide on how to design and approach a dopamine detox in ways that will encourage you to remain dedicated and secure long-term benefits.

Let's get started!

Chapter 2:
The Neuroscience of Dopamine

Dopamine, the important role player in our story, is very aptly nicknamed the "feel-good hormone" and is inarguably one of the most well-known neurotransmitters next to serotonin, the "happy hormone" and oxytocin, the "love hormone." In fact, you may have already seen dopamine's chemical structure on necklaces and clothing with its rise in fame within the more general population.

Dopamine has also been identified as one of the main characters in the brain's "reward system" and assists in motivating people by associating certain behaviors with feelings of reward.

In order to better understand how dopamine detox actually works and how to approach it in a way that is as beneficial as possible, it is imperative to first appreciate the neuroscience behind this technique and that starts with learning about dopamine and its role in reward associations.

The following sections are more scientific in nature and may be too in-depth for what you may need. Keep in mind that you don't have to perfectly understand the neuroscience behind dopamine in order to succeed with your dopamine detox.

For those of you who simply want to understand how dopamine is implicated in addictive behavior, you may skip to the sub-chapter "Dopamine Theory of Addiction" (in this chapter).

If you want to get straight to the framework and guidelines on how to make a dopamine detox work for you, you can go straight to chapter four.

You're still there? Amazing, let's dive deep into the neuroscience of dopamine!

First Things First, What is Dopamine?

Dopamine is a monoamine neurotransmitter, an endogenous chemical within the brain that allows important information to be relayed between neurons in the brain and throughout the body. When looking closer at its chemical structure, dopamine consists of an amino group bonded by a two-carbon chain to tyrosine, an aromatic ring. This structure - an amino group bonded to an aromatic ring by a two-carbon chain - is characteristic of monoamine neurotransmitters, which include serotonin, histamine, epinephrine, and norepinephrine. In fact, with the assistance of an enzyme known as beta-hydroxylase, dopamine undergoes a chemical process that results in the production of norepinephrine.

Now let's have a look at what happens between neurons; why do we need neurotransmitters?

Well, neurotransmitters are essential for synaptic transmission, which is the transfer of information between neurons. The whole process of synaptic transmission is a fascinating phenomenon as it is the driving force of all our functions, even in early embryological development.

If you were to look at a system of neurons, you would notice that they are connected with one another by junctions known as synapses and that a minuscule gap, called the synaptic cleft, exists between the axon terminal of the presynaptic neuron and the membrane of the postsynaptic neuron.

Chemical messages between neurons are transmitted from the presynaptic neuron to the postsynaptic neuron. The synaptic cleft is where the neurotransmitter and other molecules are released so they can activate a signal, referred to as an action potential, in the membrane of the postsynaptic neuron. Essentially, this action potential will be the main channel of information in the nervous system and muscles, telling the receiving neuron what neurotransmitter or molecule to release next, and depending on the neurotransmitter released, it will be determined if the action potential initiated an excitatory or inhibitory response.

There are several different neurotransmitters, and each one has important responsibilities for a range of vital functions within the brain and body. Returning to dopamine's nickname, *"the feel-good hormone"*, one might mistakenly believe that dopamine's only or most important function is creating feelings of pleasure and reward within individuals; however, this is not true at all. Dopamine is actually responsible for a whole range of functions; including executive functions, emotion, learning, reward, motivation, and motor control.

It is important to remember that neurophysiology is not as simple as saying, "neurotransmitter A is responsible for function A and neurotransmitter B is responsible for function B." Each neurotransmitter has a wide variety of functions and depending on the location and what else is happening in the body will determine what that function will be. For example, dopamine's function in the substantia nigra of the brain is predominantly related to motor control; whereas in the premotor cortex, it is responsible for executive functions like planning and inhibition.

If you were to take the term *"dopamine fast"* literally it would mean ridding your body and brain of its dopamine levels. This is not just impossible, but would also be extremely dangerous and not have the desired effect whatsoever.

Abnormal levels of dopamine have been associated with the development of certain neurological and psychiatric disorders; such as Parkinson's disease, Schizophrenia, Huntington's disease, depression, chemical/behavioral addiction, and even conditions such as restless leg syndrome.

This knowledge assists medical professionals and researchers in developing medications to help patients with these disorders; however, each condition is a bit more complicated than having too little or too much dopamine. See, neuroscience is always interesting!

Looking within the brain again, four dopaminergic pathways have been identified; namely, the nigrostriatal pathway which is involved in the planning of voluntary movement, the tuberoinfundibular pathway which aids in the inhibition of prolactin release, the mesocortical pathway which is responsible for executive functions such as working memory, decision making, and cognition, and finally the mesolimbic pathway which is associated with the function that most people think of when hearing the word "dopamine" - pleasure and reward. We will be focusing on two of the pathways for the purpose of dopamine detox; the mesocortical and mesolimbic pathways.

The Mesolimbic Pathway of Dopamine

The mesolimbic pathway begins in an area of the midbrain known as the ventral tegmental area which is rich in dopamine and extends to the nucleus accumbens, amygdala, and hippocampus of the brain. It is here at the nucleus accumbens that dopamine is released when presented with particular behaviors or stimuli that are either reinforcing or rewarding, like eating a delicious cake or looking through social media, and the brain will learn to associate the behavior or stimuli with feelings of reward or pleasure. This pathway is especially useful in motivating people to repeat certain behaviors or return to stimuli that have resulted in these feelings.

A key fact to keep in mind about dopamine is that it does not actually create feelings of pleasure or reward. The mesolimbic pathway is referred to as the reward center of the brain because it is here that particular stimuli and behaviors are associated with feelings of reward. Dopamine's responsibility does not lie in producing feelings of joy, pleasure, and reward. This has been proven in experiments where dopaminergic cell groups were destroyed in test animals, thereby resulting in no dopamine within the animal. However, even without the presence of dopamine, these animals were observed to still experience pleasure when exposed to rewarding stimuli like sucrose solutions.

The mesolimbic pathway helps your brain remember what brings you feelings of reward and pleasure so that you can seek these behaviors out again in the future as a way to replicate the good feelings. Some avoidance behaviors are rewarded and reinforced as well. This shows us that dopamine is involved in both types of reinforcement, positive and negative, and both increase the probability of repeating the behavior in the future. With negative reinforcement, the behavior results in the removal of something the individual regards as unpleasant; for example, during a period of substantial emotional distress you may keep yourself occupied by binge-watching television shows, and the unwanted negative emotions will be avoided for that time being. In this example, the behavior of watching television will be reinforced and the reward is the avoidance of uncomfortable emotions. Positive reinforcement is when a behavior or stimulus elicits a pleasant result which encourages repetition. For example, if someone begins feeling more energized after religiously drinking eight glasses of water a day for a week they may associate the reward, i.e. having more energy, with the behavior of drinking more water and repeat this.

Basically, dopamine is responsible for us acting in particular ways in order to acquire a reward or steer clear of anything that is regarded as undesirable. This is where dopamine's function in regulating motivational behavior is explained. When looking at an individual's motivation towards a goal, researchers theorize that high levels of dopamine within the mesolimbic pathway are associated with higher levels of motivation observed in some people. It is this motivation that encourages you to repeat behaviors, like getting up from the couch and fetching a soft drink from the fridge or driving to the casino to gamble.

Motivation is often extremely advantageous; for example, someone may feel motivated to clean their kitchen by subconsciously remembering how accomplished they felt previously after cleaning their space. From an evolutionary viewpoint, motivation would have been valuable for our ancestors when initiating survival behaviors such as searching for food and shelter. It is when this motivation supports maladaptive or unwanted behaviors that it becomes an issue because it aids in the repetition of them.

It has also been discovered that dopamine is sometimes released before receiving reinforcement and in some cases by just the thought of the associated behavior or stimuli, supporting the role of dopamine in motivation. This is referred to as reward anticipation and usually occurs if a particular behavior or stimulant is presented enough times to the reward system. An example of this might be if you form a daily habit of watching a particular television series as soon as you get home from work, the anticipation of relaxing and watching your favorite show will result in your brain releasing dopamine even before you have switched the television on. This is only true for extremely strong dopamine-behavior associations.

This anticipation is especially helpful during instances where you might be losing momentum while trying to achieve a goal, by thinking about the reward that you will receive after it can re-energize and motivate you to complete. For example, you may be nearly finished with a work or school project but are beginning to feel tired or stuck; anticipating the reward of having the rest of the day free to yourself when you are finished can encourage you to push through and complete your project.

Before we continue with the next pathway, let's have a quick look at the "limbic" part of the mesolimbic pathway. Both the hippocampus and amygdala are part of the limbic system, which is a collection of brain structures believed to be responsible for lower-order emotional and behavioral processing from sensory system inputs. This is especially evident in survival behaviors such as fight or flight, eating, reproduction, and care for the young. The hippocampus is largely involved in the storage of long-term memory and possibly its retrieval in some cases; whereas the amygdala is responsible for emotional memory, fear conditioning, social cognition, and strong feelings like aggression and anxiety.

The Mesocortical Pathway of Dopamine

The mesocortical pathway begins in the ventral tegmental area, just like the mesolimbic pathway, however, it projects towards the cerebral cortex where it forms profound amounts of connections with the prefrontal cortex, cingulate cortex, and entorhinal cortex. The prefrontal cortex is one of the main structures within this pathway.

The prefrontal cortex is the most anterior section of the frontal lobe and lies in front of the premotor cortex and right behind the eyes. It is one of the final brain areas to experience complete myelination during adolescence and spans about one-third of the cerebral cortex. It is believed that the prefrontal cortex is fully developed by the age of twenty-five.

Unfortunately, most of our knowledge surrounding the functions of brain structures is prompted by clinical cases in which these structures have been damaged or impaired in some way. The story leading up to the discovery of the prefrontal cortex's functions is no different and is possibly one of the most interesting cases. On September 13, 1848, a significant date within the neuroscience realm, a railroad construction foreman, Phineas Gage, was involved in a horrifying accident that resulted in an iron rod being driven into his left cheek, through his brain, and out his skull. Miraculously, not only did Gage survive this terrible incident but he remained conscious throughout and was able to call someone for help. Over time, however, it was determined that he had not remained the same person he was before the accident. He was now observed to be much more impulsive and socially inappropriate.

Gage's accident was a substantial stepping stone and he is often referred to as "the man who began neuroscience" because his case helped support the localization theory of the brain; the belief that particular parts of the brain are associated with specific functions. Almost two hundred years on and we now have a much better understanding of the prefrontal cortex's functions, which do not begin and end at personality. It is responsible for cognitive analysis, supervising socially appropriate behaviors, intelligence, language, memory, abstract thought, executive functions, and practicing good judgment. All essential functions, but its role in executive functions is what we are going to focus on.

Executive functions refer to a collection of skills involved in planning complex behaviors, decision-making, achieving goals that have been set, remaining focused on a task at hand, and the expression of self-regulation which includes the control of impulsive behaviors. These skills develop right after birth and continue through adolescence and the young adult years with the peak development occurring in the mid-twenties. This method of development may point to why adolescents and younger adults are more prone to addictive behaviors.

Dopamine Theory of Addiction

In the 1890s, Ivan Pavlov accidentally discovered that dogs were able to display a conditioned response after being exposed to a previously neutral stimulus. He first trained the dogs by ringing a bell (the neutral stimulus) and then immediately feeding them (the unconditioned stimulus), which resulted in them salivating (unconditioned response). Once he had determined that an association had been made, he removed the unconditioned stimulus, i.e. the food, but kept the bell. Pavlov observed that the dogs would salivate at the sound of the bell alone, thus concluding that they had been conditioned to anticipate food when hearing the bell. This is a form of learning known as classical conditioning where certain stimuli are paired with neutral stimuli to eventually elicit a particular behavior from the neutral stimuli. Humans display similar anticipatory behaviors and looking inside the brain, researchers have proposed an interesting theory about dopamine.

It was the year 1954, and Peter Milner and James Olds just made a huge discovery in the world of neuroscience. In a study conducted on rats, some of the best teachers when it comes to behavior studies, they stimulated an area in some rats' brains using an electrical current and discovered that this stimulation resulted in the rats repeating a particular activity. When researched further they discovered that dopamine was involved which led to the conclusion that dopamine has something to do with enjoyment.

Remember signal transduction? A presynaptic neuron causes the release of neurotransmitters into the synaptic cleft which initiates an action potential in the postsynaptic neuron. When a stimulus or behavior is overexerted and there is chronic usage, the postsynaptic neuron will begin downregulating the signal by becoming less sensitive to dopamine. This is the brain's way of attempting to establish some sort of equilibrium. However, this also means that much more dopamine is required in order to produce the same level of enjoyment.

Another problem that arises in this situation is that other activities, especially sources of natural dopamine-stimulating behaviors, feel much less pleasurable. For example, people who have downregulated dopamine receptors may find it difficult to read or enjoy time in nature.

When a rewarding behavior or stimulus is encountered, there is competition between the mesolimbic and mesocortical pathways, with the mesolimbic pathway fighting to receive more rewarding stimuli and the mesocortical pathway trying to inhibit this behavior. Someone with optimal mesocorticolimbic functioning will have an adequate balance between the two pathways, but for someone with defective functions in the pathways, their balance will tip to one side.

When someone regularly seeks out high dopamine activities there is a chance that their mesolimbic pathway will overtake their mesocortical pathway. This will cause impairment in their ability to plan out behaviors and they will exhibit problems with inhibition. Therefore you will have someone that is continuously turning towards stimuli and behaviors that will give them instantaneous gratification, often finding it difficult to stop themselves or turn their attention towards more important tasks at hand. They will also experience difficulty engaging in behaviors that are not immediately rewarding.

Another observed implication of this is that people with disrupted neurons in the nucleus accumbens will have an impairment in their effort computation. They will only be able to choose activities that require low effort and give them a low reward; their motivation is towards quick forms of reward.

The Modern World's Role in Excessive Dopamine Release

For many of us, it may be difficult, or even impossible depending on our age, to remember when cell phones were not a common item in households and on our person. However, there was a time when humans did not know what a smartphone notification was, nevermind what it looked or sounded like. Throughout the years since their invention, these notifications have become a conditioned stimulus, much like the bell for Pavlov's dogs, that elicits anticipation for the reward of reading a message, temporarily alleviating any negative emotions, or busying oneself by watching the latest episode of a riveting television show.

Double reinforcement may potentially occur where the excitement of reading the notification acts as a positive reinforcement and the easing up of negative feelings, such as stress, anxiety, or boredom, acts as a negative reinforcement of the behavior. This has the ability to encourage behaviors that may be regarded as addictive or impulsive because they will distract away from life's problems and bring a feeling of pleasure while also numbing any unwanted and uncomfortable emotions. Sounds inviting, doesn't it? Unfortunately, this is the beginning of a spiral into a life of empty rewards and meaningless behaviors.

Chapter 3:
The Benefits of Doing a Dopamine Detox

The primary advertised benefit of dopamine detox is that you will become less reliant on addictive behaviors and stimuli which could be messing substantially with your dopaminergic pathway functioning. Your brain will be allowed to find enjoyment in the more simple things. In addition to this, supporters also believe that dopamine detox can benefit your mental and physical health. Many people who have gone on a dopamine detox have described feeling so much better, with an increased focus on the more important things in life and energy to accomplish their goals.

Potential Benefits on Your Mental and Physical Health.

Dr. Sepah has stated that his technique of dopamine detox is based on common approaches used in cognitive behavioral therapy (CBT). CBT is a form of talk therapy used by many mental health professionals and is concerned with the connection between emotions, thoughts, and behaviors. Therapists use this treatment approach to guide their clients on how to develop coping mechanisms that are healthy. They are also encouraged to practically become their own therapists outside of their sessions. Therefore we can deduce that the benefits observed in clients who undergo CBT will also take place during a dopamine detox.

CBT encourages the improvement of mindfulness and a common CBT technique that Dr. Sepah suggests is stimulus control. This approach encourages the client to connect a pattern of behavior with the presence of a particular stimulus and identify the trigger. Another CBT technique proposed is urge surfing where an individual works on mindfulness and is encouraged to become aware of the impulses surrounding the compulsive behavior and sit with these feelings for a while. This will help them to control their impulses better and helps immensely in preventing relapse. These forms of CBT are well studied and provide an individual with opportunities to reflect on the behavior, what is causing it, and how to be encouraged to turn to healthier behaviors.

By limiting the dopamine-heavy stimuli, we are allowing our brain to quieten down and not be so overwhelmed by the "noise" of constant dopamine hits. This will allow you to be more present with yourself and feel emotions you may have been bottling up. After a dopamine detox, people have described feeling clarity about situations in their life or decisions they had to make. When people consciously restrict addictive behaviors they become more aware of how impulsive it is and they are encouraged to think more flexibly.

Repairing the mesolimbic pathway's functioning allows it to reestablish balance with the mesocortical pathway. When these two pathways are better in tune with one another again, those functions that were impaired will begin to perform satisfactorily again. Therefore an individual's ability to plan out and execute tasks will improve, as will their concentration when working and completing important projects. Dr. Sepah argues that by developing a "time-restricted pleasure," you are training yourself to use your time and energy more wisely and decrease procrastination, further improving this pathway balance.

From a neurophysiology perspective, dopamine detox allows the readaptation of the neurochemistry and the neurons to produce new cellular machinery. This is based on the principles and understanding of neuroscience. When their levels of dopamine are at an optimal balance, an individual will feel motivated, happy, focused, and attentive; however, when their levels are low it may cause fatigue, decreased motivation, mood swings, unhappiness, concentration issues, sleep difficulties, and memory loss.

Not only does dopamine detox benefit your mental well-being, but it also has proposed physical health benefits. People who are stuck in a pattern of compulsive behaviors are often so absorbed by them that they are not able to find the time to partake in physical activity like exercising. This is especially true for addictive behaviors like excessive internet usage, watching hours of television, and gaming. All these activities encourage someone to remain sedentary. Moving your body has been proven beneficial for both physical and mental health. As we will see later, dopamine detox encourages certain behaviors like exercise and cooking for yourself which improve your healthy living. The exercise suggested does not have to be intense, but rather gentler forms like yoga and walking.

Scientific Evidence of Dopamine Detox's Effects on the Brain.

Although Dr. Sepah has referred to his technique as "evidence-based," it is important to note that no randomized clinical trials have been published that prove a dopamine detox actually works, and therefore not much is known about its physiological effect on the brain. What reports we do have is from Dr. Sepah himself and his endorsement of this technique as well as the many testimonials from people who have gone on a dopamine detox. This lack of scientific evidence is understandable as the technique is still in its very, very early years and research studies take both time and money to publish results that are valid and reliable.

A literature review on dopamine detox was published in 2021 where they concluded that as long as the detoxer is aware of the misconceptions surrounding this technique and remains clear of it, it can be a highly effective approach to regaining power over rewarding behaviors. They recommend that more studies should be conducted to determine how safe and effective self-guided dopamine detox is.

Even though there isn't scientific evidence proving dopamine detox itself, there are studies proving the validity of CBT, which, as we know, dopamine detox is highly based on. CBT has both scientific evidence and clinical practice to back its relevancy and has been found to be highly reliable in motivating change within the individual's patterns of thought and behavior. CBT is used to treat a whole host of mental disorders such as anxiety disorders, mood disorders, eating disorders, as well as addictions, and even instances of relationship problems. Studies report that CBT is as effective, sometimes even more so, when compared to other therapeutic approaches and psychiatric medications as clients are taught to recognize and be proactive about undesirable behaviors. Studies have also shown that it is especially useful when working to resist compulsive behaviors and avoid relapses.

Thus, with this in mind we can see that using the principles of CBT as its foundation, dopamine detox definitely has some scientific relevance to it. It just has to be well understood so that it can be done correctly. Because this approach has been adopted by many people who are wanting to implement behavioral changes by themselves, including a mental health professional in their detox plan is often not considered. This is alright in cases where the restricted stimuli or behavior will not result in any life-threatening withdrawals, like giving up shopping or social media usage, but it is not recommended in situations where the addictive behavior involves substances like drugs or alcohol.

When someone uses excessive amounts of alcohol or other drugs, they might experience symptoms of alcohol withdrawal that can range anywhere from sweating and headaches to delirium tremens, violent seizures, and even death. The severity of these symptoms highly depends on what they are giving up, their age, underlying medical issues, and how long they have been addicted to the substance. Other common effects of sudden alcohol withdrawal in people who have been addicted for a long time are an electrolyte imbalance, dehydration, and malnutrition which may lead to something known as Wernicke-Korsakoff syndrome. Wernicke-Korsakoff syndrome involves Wenicke's encephalopathy, which is a dangerous but short-term condition involving issues with muscle coordination, confusion, and paralysis of the optic nerve. It also may involve Korsakoff's psychosis, which is a more long-term condition that results in learning and long-term memory impairment.

Therefore, in some instances, it is imperative to consult with a medical professional that understands the potential risks before embarking on dopamine detox. They will assist with safe methods to curb addictive behaviors and guide on the best method to use.

Chapter 4:
Proven Strategies for an Effective Dopamine Detox

So, you have read about the proposed benefits of dopamine detox and are ready to get started. What is the best approach to beginning a detox and which stimuli or behaviors should you limit?

First of all, how can you determine if you are really in need of a dopamine detox?

Identify if you are exhibiting any compulsive behaviors that are not actually enjoyable. This is a distinctive pattern where the mesolimbic pathway is pushing the behavior but is receiving tolerance to enjoyment; essentially the reinforcement exists but the resulting reward is very small. Next, if you are finding it difficult to enjoy simple activities like going for a walk or listening to music, it may be another indication that you will benefit from a dopamine detox. Finally, if you are finding that you are conflicted between what you know you should be doing and the compulsive behavior, with the compulsive behavior winning most of the time, you are definitely in need of a dopamine detox.

Going into a dopamine detox, you need to keep in mind that it will not be easy. You are placing yourself in situations where you will have no distractions, ultimately leaving you to feel those emotions you have been trying to avoid or having to face certain tough decisions. In addition to this, you will also be surrounded by the things you are restricting yourself from, which may definitely make it more difficult to remain dedicated to the detox. I would say that you need to begin your dopamine detox with motivation, but we have seen how motivation can be destroyed by instantaneous gratification from the very things you are avoiding.

Although it may seem as though the odds are stacked against you, don't lose heart! This chapter is going to guide you on how to best modify your detox so that it can serve you well and benefit you throughout and after. See this as an encouraging best friend, holding your hand and guiding you through your goals towards better mental health and a more fulfilling life.

How to Approach a Dopamine Detox.

Before beginning your dopamine detox journey, you must recognize precisely which stimuli you need to fast from. Dr. Sepah offers a list of possible addictions as guidance, however, he does note that this is neither exclusive nor inclusive. Many things around us have the potential to become addictive, it is our responsibility to identify them.

Again keeping the three features of a problematic stimulus in mind; is it addictive, impairing my life, and/or causing me distress?

Recognizing the troubling stimuli is not as simple as just identifying which compulsive behavior to limit, but also the reward promoting this behavior, and any triggers. This refers back to the CBT technique known as stimulus control that Dr. Sepah suggests. Let's go through each one of these.

First you are going to determine exactly which stimuli and behaviors are compulsive; do you reach for your phone and scroll through social media almost automatically or do you find yourself eating ice cream but not actually enjoying it? These are the questions you need to ask so that you can recognize exactly what you need to cut out or limit. Next, you need to determine what the reward is that drives the compulsive behavior. For example, eating the ice cream might be taking you away from your work, giving you a much-needed break that you otherwise would have skipped. So is the reward a result of eating the ice cream or is it because your brain has associated ice cream with taking a break? This is where you need to bring in a journal and write down how you feel so that the reward can be easily identified. Finally, are there any triggers to these behaviors and the need for a reward? Possible triggers are the time, location, emotional state, other people, or an immediately preceding action. Do you find yourself reaching for your phone only when in the company of certain people, or do you shop more often when experiencing emotions of sadness and hopelessness?

This may all seem like a lot of work, but dopamine detox is inherently filled with opportunities for self-reflection which is always beneficial.

Once you have completed this first step and decided on what you want to limit, you will need to deduce the time period of your dopamine detox. This will solely depend on you, your lifestyle, and what you are limiting. Dr. Sepah suggests starting small and in ways that cause as little disruption to your daily functioning as possible. This is to encourage compliance with your detox plan and avoid you feeling overwhelmed in staying true to your goals. However, twenty-four to seventy-two hours, which is the recommended time period by many people advocating for dopamine detox, is not near enough time to mend dopamine receptor regulation. You want to give your brain the opportunity to upregulate its dopamine receptors, and this process of restoring receptor regulation requires at least two weeks before it shows any signs of working. A successful dopamine detox can last up to twelve weeks.

Because quitting some addictive behaviors cold turkey can be challenging, Dr. Sepah proposes to systematically limit the behaviors or stimuli. This will still lead to the behavioral plasticity that you are looking for and can eventually guide you toward increasing the restriction period to at least two weeks. Suppose you identified social media usage as the behavior you want to restrict, but you feel like giving it up for two weeks will not be possible. Begin with limiting your time on social media to one hour a day, possibly only every second day, then increase this limit by abstaining from social media for one whole day every week, finally, you can then restrict all forms of social media for at least two weeks.

How to Tailor Your Dopamine Detox to Your Personal Goals and Needs.

So what should you do during your dopamine detox? Supporters of this approach recommend engaging in activities that reflect your interests and values, that way you are more likely to remain dedicated to them. These should be activities that elicit natural forms of dopamine release and benefit you in some way.

Some suggested activities to include in your plan are meditation, exercise, daily walks, practicing a new or existing skill, in-person social gatherings like a board game night or quiz night, cooking, reading, listening to podcasts that encourage learning, road trips or camping, hiking, journaling, and getting involved in community projects where you can help others.

All these take you away from high dopamine activities and instead offer you opportunities to increase your motivation and reflect on yourself, your life, and your emotions. For example, going camping will stimulate your mesocortical pathway which will start improving your organization skills, journaling will help you recognize your emotions better and can be used to reflect on your detox journey, spending time on a hobby can motivate you and socializing will strengthen relationships that may have been damaged due to your addictive behavior.

All the above are examples of simple activities that anyone can participate in for some time during the detox and will increase levels of dopamine in healthier, natural ways.

Another important factor to keep in mind is the nature of what you are limiting. For example, if you have identified internet usage as a destructive habit that you want to limit but you predominantly work from home online, you need to keep this in mind when planning your detox schedule. Therefore, you may not be able to "fast" from the internet every day, possibly only during the weekend or for an hour every second day. Your goals must be realistic and still beneficial to your daily life.

How to Stay Dedicated to Your Dopamine Detox.

The biggest obstacle to a dopamine detox is boredom. Not only will you be bored from not being able to partake in your usual activities, but normal, simple activities that should be enjoyable will not be; especially during the early stages. That is why it is highly recommended to plan out your day. This will act as a handy weapon against boredom and is a wonderful opportunity to get your mesocortical pathway working more.

If possible you can plan out each day before starting your detox otherwise you could also plan the next day's activities before going to bed. Try your best to fill the day up as much as possible because unstructured time can become your worst enemy during a dopamine detox. When your mind is bored, it is much easier for the restricted behavior to sneak its way back in. You can also use this planning time to download audiobooks and podcasts to keep you busy during relatively boring activities like washing the dishes, folding laundry, and cleaning the house. You can download movies, about three movies for two weeks, but no streaming services as this would allow binge-watching. Video games as well as an accumulation of content and information should also be avoided during this period.

Another strategy that will help you remain dedicated is to make the restricted stimuli as inaccessible as possible. If you are restricting internet or social media usage, log out and delete all apps from your digital devices. Install internet blockers to inhibit you from accessing restricted sites and delete streaming services.

Taking the detox with family and/or friends is a wonderful strategy to keep you motivated and hold you accountable. This is a great way to support and encourage one another because you are all restricting the behavior together. Dopamine detox may feel lonely if you are partaking by yourself, especially if you see your family or friends enjoying what you have limited for yourself. It also affords the opportunity for you to discuss your personal experiences regarding the detox with one another. This may bring more insight into the internal mental state of those around you, hopefully leading to more understanding and compassion. You can all participate in hobbies together and spend time in nature, offering you more socialization.

Chapter 5:
Maintaining the Long-term Benefits

You've just gone through a dopamine detox and are feeling so much better, but what happens now? How do you reintroduce the restricted stimulus or behavior and how can you maintain the benefits experienced in the long term?

How to Maintain Long-term Benefits

American psychiatrist, Dr. Anna Lembke, is a strong advocate for dopamine detox especially in restricting addictive internet and social media usage. Dr. Lembke mentions that an individual can approach the behavior or stimulus with full or partial avoidance. This will depend on your discoveries made while detoxing and the nature of what you are restricting. For example, alcohol and other drugs will more than likely require complete abstinence, but social media will be partial. Dr. Lembke proposes three strategies that she refers to as "self-binding strategies" which can be used to sustain the healthy relationship with high-dopamine activities that you will acquire by detoxing. These refer to space, time, and category.

Beginning with the space, this refers to establishing barriers in relation to the restricted stimulus. Examples of this are similar to what you would have done during dopamine detox; put your phone out of reach, don't store an overabundance of junk food at home, etc. This will make the stimulus less accessible. Next is the time strategy which involves limiting the time you use the stimulus. Decide if you are limiting this to certain hours per day or to a certain day each week. This would include downloading programs that limit screen time on your phone or computer which lets you know you have reached your limit for the day or deciding on how many hours per week you are allowed to shop. The hope is that you will be able to use the mindful and impulse control skills gained during the detox to remain dedicated to your time limit. Finally, we have the categorical strategy, where you devote the behavior or stimulus to a particular occasion or setting. For example, limit eating cake only for birthdays or other celebrations.

Additional Lifestyle Changes Supporting the Benefits of a Dopamine Detox

In addition to Dr. Lembke's strategies, there are some more approaches that sustain dopamine detox values.

Many people believe that how you spend your morning, especially how you start the morning, will determine the rest of the day. This is what inspired the trend of low dopamine mornings, an approach originally advised for people with ADHD.

The idea of a low-dopamine morning is to begin your day with as few high-dopamine sources as possible. This means not reaching for your phone or not drinking coffee first thing after waking up and rather participating in simple activities like sitting in the morning sun for a few minutes or meditating. Studies have shown that scrolling through social media or reading emails first thing in the morning sets up for a stressful day. You will feel busy before even getting out of bed, which has also been shown to affect productivity throughout the day. It is recommended that you avoid high-dopamine activities for at least one hour in the morning.

This low dopamine schedule can be extended to your nighttime routine as well as a way to quieten your mind after a long, busy day and have a good night's rest. This is referred to as "sleep hygiene" and involves switching off all screens an hour before bed and reading a book, journaling, or doing sleep-time yoga.

Another way to ensure you receive long-term benefits from the detox is to reflect on your journal accounts written during the detox period. This is why journaling throughout this journey is so important! Having records of how you felt before the detox, during, and after is a superb way to remind yourself of all the work you have put in and how much you have accomplished. It also allows you to relate similar feelings you may be experiencing in the present and identify if you may need to dopamine detox again soon.

This brings us to - repeating the dopamine detox. If dopamine detox was beneficial for you, it may be worthwhile repeating the dopamine detox in a few months' time. In fact, many people detox every quarter or twice a year. Repeating dopamine detox does not mean that you did it wrong the first time or are not remaining dedicated to your goals, it is just another way to reinforce the healthy relationship you have established with the behavior or stimulus.

Chapter 6:
Conclusion

In summary, dopamine detox may not have clinical trials backing its validity just yet, but its foundation in CBT principles supports the claims that it is beneficial in defeating addictive behaviors and promoting better relationships with compulsive behaviors.

Summary of the Benefits and Strategies Discussed

Partaking in dopamine detox is beneficial for your mental health, physical health, and neurophysiology. Some of its proposed benefits include improving mood, productivity, relationships, and motivation. The consensus from people who have undergone dopamine detox is that these, and other improvements are seen in their life. A neurophysiological benefit is in the re-establishment of dopamine receptors to their baseline levels. This also allows for the mesocorticolimbic pathway relationship to be in sync again resulting in optimal functioning.

 Whether you decide on a partial or full dopamine detox is up to you and your situation, but it is highly recommended to completely restrict the stimulus for at least two weeks. Even if this means starting small and slowly building yourself up to full abstinence. Your dopamine detox journey is individual to you and you should plan it as such, allowing yourself flexibility where it is needed.

We also covered some strategies meant to assist you in remaining dedicated and benefiting from all this work in the long term. It also will help to do a dopamine detox with family and friends, as well as get a mental health professional involved if necessary.

Final Thoughts on the Potential Impact of Dopamine Detox

Given the attention it deserves from the scientific community, dopamine detox may be a valuable psychological intervention in helping people regain control over their lives. Our modern world is filled with numerous sources of instantaneous gratification and the best way to limit these in our lives is by becoming aware of them and forming healthy relationships with them so that we can be proactive if they start becoming addictive or compulsive. This is why dopamine detox may be so beneficial for our society as a whole.

As Dr. Anna Lembke said: *"it's the things we do before being met with temptations that prepare us to withstand unhealthy urges."*

One Final Note

Dear Reader,

I'm Andrew Humington, the author of this book.

Writing this book was both challenging and enjoyable, and I genuinely hope you've gained valuable insights from our time together.

Before we part ways, I'd like to share something important:

As a self-published author, I don't have the backing of a large publishing house with extensive advertising budgets or widespread promotional campaigns.

This book stems from my passion for neuroscience and my desire to share its findings to benefit as many people as possible.

I sincerely hope it helps you fulfill your potential.

Now, it's my turn to request a small favor from you:

If this book has been helpful to you and you believe it could benefit others, please consider leaving a review by clicking the link below or visiting amazon.com.

Reviews are vital for us, as they help prevent our book from being lost in the vast sea of Amazon rankings and ensure it remains visible to potential readers.

Your completion of this book is already more than I could ask for, but if you could spare just a minute to leave a review on Amazon, it would mean the world to me.

Regardless, thank you once again for placing your trust in me and giving this book a chance.

If you're interested in learning more about recent neuroscience discoveries and how they can help you transform your life, I plan to publish additional works on various topics within the NeuroEducation Lab collection (available on Amazon and Audible).

I hope to see you there!

Wishing you a fantastic day, and a heartfelt thank you if you decide to leave a review.

Andrew Humington

References

(2008). Adaptation of Sensory Receptors. In: Binder, M.D., Hirokawa, N., Windhorst, U. (eds) *Encyclopedia of Neuroscience*. Springer, Berlin, Heidelberg. https://doi.org/10.1007/978-3-540-29678-2_86

After Skool. (2020, August 4). Dopamine fasting 2.0 - overcome addiction & restore motivation [Video file]. Retrieved from https://www.youtube.com/watch?v=jCWADjUA9il

Alexander, G.E., DeLong, M.R. & Strick, P.L. (1986, March). Parallel organization of functionally segregated circuits linking basal ganglia and cortex. *Annual Review of Neuroscience, 9*, 357-381. https://doi.org/10.1146/annurev.ne.09.030186.002041

Allen, R. (2004, July). Dopamine and iron in the pathophysiology of restless legs syndrome (RLS). *Sleep Medicine, 5*(4), 385-391. https://doi.org/10.1016/j.sleep.2004.01.012

Asociación RUVID. (2013, January 10). Dopamine regulates the motivation to act, study shows. *ScienceDaily*. Retrieved from https://www.sciencedaily.com/releases/2013/01/130110094415.htm

AtlasBioMed. (2023, February 18). Dopamine detox: what is it, how do you do it and does it work? Retrieved from https://atlasbiomed.com/blog/dopamine-detox-what-is-it-how-do-you-do-it-and-does-it-work/

Bastian, J. (2022, October 8). Dopamine nation: living in an addicted world [Web log post]. Retrieved from https://www.kcrw.com/culture/shows/life-examined/anna-lembke-dopamine-nation-addiction-pleasure-opioids-fentanyl#:~:text=Lembke%20often%20recommends%20that%20her,you%20feel%20after%20a%20month.

Berry, J. & Han, S. (2023, January 12). What are neurotransmitters? [Web log post]. Retrieved from https://www.medicalnewstoday.com/articles/326649

Blaess, S., Stott, S.R.W. & Ang, S.L. (2020). The generation of midbrain dopaminergic neurons. In J. Rubenstein, B. Chen, P. Rakic & K.Y. Kwan (Eds.), *Patterning and Cell Type Specification in the Developing CNS and PNS* (pp. 369-398). Academic Press. https://doi.org/10.1016/B978-0-12-814405-3.00017-5

Bridges, N. (2016, November 25). Dopamine pathways. Retrieved from https://sanescohealth.com/blog/dopamine-pathways/

Calbet, J. (2020, January 20). Dopamine fasting technique seen from neuroquotient [Web log post]. Retrieved from https://neuroquotient.com/en/dopamine-fasting-technique-seen-from-neuroquotient/

Chan, O. (2023, February 11). Could a dopamine detox help you be more productive this year? [Web log post]. Retrieved from https://freedom.to/blog/dopamine-detox/#:~:text=These%20activities%20reduce%20stress%2C%20improve,need%20or%20truly%20want%20to.

Chen, A. (2018, March 27). Please stop calling dopamine the pleasure chemical [Web log post]. Retrieved from https://www.theverge.com/2018/3/27/17169446/dopamine-pleasure-chemical-neuroscience-reward-motivation

Cherry, K. (2022, November 11). How negative reinforcement works [Web log post]. Retrieved from https://www.verywellmind.com/what-is-negative-reinforcement-2795410

Fei, Y.Y., Johnson, P.A., Omran, N.A.L, Mardon, A. & Johnson, J.C. (2021, December 11). Maladaptive or misunderstood? Dopamine fasting as a potential intervention for behavioral addiction. *Lifestyle Medicine, 3*(1). https://doi.org/10.1002/lim2.54

Fletcher, S. (2019, December 5). A natural high: Healthy ways to boost dopamine. Retrieved from https://canadiancentreforaddictions.org/a-natural-high-healthy-ways-to-boost dopamine/#:~:text=Certain%20drugs%20(such%20as%20alcohol,our%20health%20and%20well%2Dbeing.

Game Quitters. How to do a dopamine detox. Retrieved from https://gamequitters.com/how-to-do-a-dopamine-detox/#:~:text=Cameron%20Sepah%20created%20the%20original,social%20media%20and%20phone%20notifications.

Gillette, H. & Olele, I. (2023, January 27). What is dopamine fasting? [Web log post] Retrieved from https://psychcentral.com/blog/dopamine-fasting-probably-doesnt-work-try-this-instead

Graff-Guerrero, A., Mizrahi, R., Agid, O., Marcon, H., Barsoum, P., Rusjan, P., Wilson, A. A., Zipursky, R. & Kapur, S. (2009). The dopamine D2 receptors in high-affinity state and D3 receptors in schizophrenia: a clinical [11C]-(+)-PHNO PET study. *Neuropsychopharmacology : official publication of the American College of Neuropsychopharmacology, 34*(4), 1078–1086. https://doi.org/10.1038/npp.2008.199

Grider MH, Jessu R, Kabir R. Physiology, Action Potential. [Updated 2022 May 15]. In: StatPearls [Internet]. Treasure Island (FL): StatPearls Publishing; 2022 Jan-. Available from: https://www.ncbi.nlm.nih.gov/books/NBK538143/

Grinspoon, P. (2020, February 26). Dopamine fasting: misunderstanding science spawns a maladaptive fad [Web log post]. Retrieved from https://www.health.harvard.edu/blog/dopamine-fasting-misunderstanding-science-spawns-a-maladaptive-fad-2020022618917

Hartley, T., Bird, C. M., Chan, D., Cipolotti, L., Husain, M., Vargha-Khadem, F. & Burgess, N. (2007). The hippocampus is required for short-term topographical memory in humans. *Hippocampus, 17*(1), 34–48. https://doi.org/10.1002/hipo.20240

HealthyGamerGG. (2021, June 12). How to stop wasting time on internet [Video file]. Retrieved from https://www.youtube.com/watch?v=RPzV8fWmKPY

HealthyGamerGG. (2021, June 8). Psychiatrist debunks dopamine fasting [Video file]. Retrieved from https://www.youtube.com/watch?v=wK-s2qBU40A

Hussain LS, Reddy V, Maani CV. Physiology, Noradrenergic Synapse. [Updated 2022 May 8]. In: StatPearls [Internet]. Treasure Island (FL): StatPearls Publishing; 2022 Jan-. Available from: https://www.ncbi.nlm.nih.gov/books/NBK540977/

Jamie. (2021, March 1). ADHD morning routines that boost dopamine part 2 [web log post]. Retrieved from https://www.addvantagehypnotherapy.co.uk/adhd-morning-routines-boost-dopamine/

Kamphuis, G. (2017, February 12). *A 40 Day Dopamine Fast.* Retrieved from
https://www.goodreads.com/en/book/show/34385485

Ko, J. H. & Strafella, A. P. (2012). Dopaminergic neurotransmission in the human brain: new lessons from perturbation and imaging. *The Neuroscientist: a review journal bringing neurobiology, neurology and psychiatry, 18*(2), 149–168. https://doi.org/10.1177/1073858411401413

Lapish, C. C., Kroener, S., Durstewitz, D., Lavin, A. & Seamans, J. K. (2007). The ability of the mesocortical dopamine system to operate in distinct temporal modes. *Psychopharmacology, 191*(3), 609–625.
https://doi.org/10.1007/s00213-006-0527-8

Linnet J. (2014). Neurobiological underpinnings of reward anticipation and outcome evaluation in gambling disorder. *Frontiers in behavioral neuroscience*, 8, 100.
https://doi.org/10.3389/fnbeh.2014.00100

MacDowell, R. (2022, May 11). Stimulus control therapy [Web log post]. Retrieved from
https://sleepopolis.com/education/stimulus-control-therapy/

Mcleod, S. (2023, February 9). Pavlov's dogs study and pavlovian conditioning explained [web log post]. Retrieved from
https://simplypsychology.org/pavlov.html

Ohwovoriole, T. (2022, October 17). 7 Natural ways to increase your dopamine levels [Web log post]. Retrieved from
https://www.verywellmind.com/natural-ways-to-increase-your-dopamine-levels-5120223

Pariyadath, V., Gowin, J.L. & Stein, E.A. (2016). Resting state functional connectivity analysis for addiction medicine: From individual loci to complex networks. In H. Ekhtiari & M.P. Paulus (Eds.), *Neuroscience for Addiction Medicine: From Prevention to Rehabilitation - Methods and Interventions* (pp. 155-173). https://doi.org/10.1016/bs.pbr.2015.07.015

Purves D, Augustine GJ, Fitzpatrick D, et al., editors. *Neuroscience. 2nd edition*. Sunderland (MA): Sinauer Associates; 2001. Excitatory and Inhibitory Postsynaptic Potentials. Available from: https://www.ncbi.nlm.nih.gov/books/NBK11117/

Salamone, J.D. & Correa, M. (2012). The mysterious motivational functions of mesolimbic dopamine. *Neuron, 76*(3), 470-485. https://doi: 10.1016/j.neuron.2012.10.021

Salimpoor, V.N, Benovoy, M., Larcher, K., Dagher, A. & Zatorre, R.J. (2011, January 9). Anatomically distinct dopamine release during anticipation and experience of peak emotion to music. *Nature Neuroscience 14*, 257–262 (2011). https://doi.org/10.1038/nn.2726

Sepah, C. The definitive guide to dopamine fasting 2.0: the hot silicon valley trend [web log post]. Retrieved from https://medium.com/swlh/dopamine-fasting-2-0-the-hot-silicon-valley-trend-7c4dc3ba2213#:~:text=The%20Definitive%20Guide%20to%20Dopamine%20Fasting%202.0%3A%20The%20Hot%20Silicon%20Valley%20Trend,-Dr.&text=Dopamine%20Fasting%202.0%20is%20an,order%20to%20regain%20behavioral%20flexibility

Sheffler Z.M., Reddy V. & Pillarisetty L.S. Physiology, Neurotransmitters. [Updated 2022 May 8]. In: StatPearls

[Internet]. Treasure Island (FL): StatPearls Publishing; 2022 Jan-. Available from: https://www.ncbi.nlm.nih.gov/books/NBK539894/

Strier, K.B. (2022). Behavioral Flexibility. In Vonk, J., Shackelford, T.K. (eds,), *Encyclopedia of Animal Cognition and Behavior*. Springer, Cham. https://doi.org/10.1007/978-3-319-55065-7_1570

Teles R. V. (2020, December). Phineas Gage's great legacy. *Dementia & neuropsychologia, 14*(4), 419–421. https://doi.org/10.1590/1980-57642020dn14-040013

Todd, L. & Gepp, K. (2021, June 29). What to know about a dopamine detox. Retrieved from https://www.medicalnewstoday.com/articles/dopamine-detox#:~:text=A%20dopamine%20detox%20entails%20fasting,evidence%20to%20support%20this%20method.

Volkow, N. D., Wang, G. J., Fowler, J. S., Tomasi, D., Telang, F. & Baler, R. (2010). Addiction: decreased reward sensitivity and increased expectation sensitivity conspire to overwhelm the brain's control circuit. *BioEssays : news and reviews in molecular, cellular and developmental biology, 32*(9), 748–755. https://doi.org/10.1002/bies.201000042

Wallisch, P. (2013, November 18). Synaptic transmission. In P. Wallisch, M.E. Lusignan, M.D. Benayoun, T.I. Baker, A.S. Dickey & N.G. Hatsopoulos (Eds.), *MATLAB for Neuroscientists (Second Ed)* (pp. 395-402). Academic Press. https://doi.org/10.1016/B978-0-12-383836-0.00026-6

Watkins, M., Generes, W.M. & Thomas, S. (2023, January 30). Risks & dangers of quitting alcohol cold turkey [Web log post]. Retrieved from https://americanaddictioncenters.org/withdrawal-timelines-treatments/cold-turkey

West, E.A., Moschak, T.M. & Carelli, R.M. (2018, August 31). Distinct functional microcircuits in the nucleus accumbens underlying goal-directed decision-making. In R. Morris, A. Bornstein & A. Shenhav. (Eds.), *Goal-Directed Decision Making* (pp. 199-219). Academic Press. https://doi.org/10.1016/B978-0-12-812098-9.00009-7

Williamson, C. (2022, August 3). Does dopamine detoxing actually work? - Andrew Huberman [Video file]. Retrieved from https://www.youtube.com/watch?v=w8pg-4c0j3s

Wise, R.A. & Jordan, C.J. (2021, December 21). Dopamine, behavior, and addiction. *Journal of Biomedical Science, 28*(83). https://doi.org/10.1186/s12929-021-00779-7

Young K. S. (2013). Treatment outcomes using CBT-IA with Internet-addicted patients. *Journal of behavioral addictions, 2*(4), 209–215. https://doi.org/10.1556/JBA.2.2013.4.3

Made in the USA
Monee, IL
20 May 2025

17841990R10030